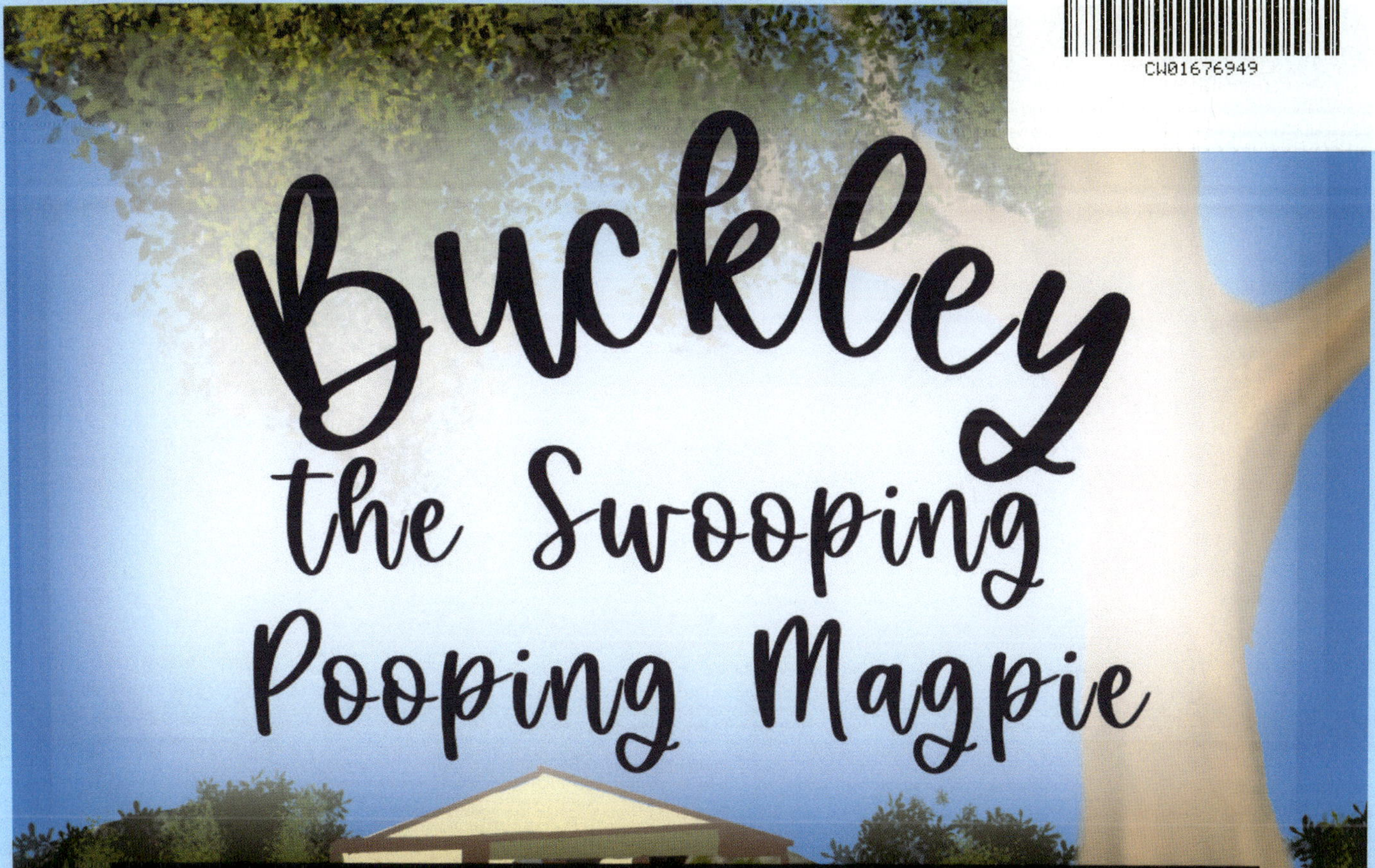

Buckley the Swooping Pooping Magpie

Written and illustrated by Lynne Edwards -
GroovyTeaching
Mount Martha, Victoria, Australia
groovyteaching@gmail.com

Cover and illustrations by Lynne Edwards

ISBN: 978-0-6454847-6-2
First Edition

Buckley the Magpie lives up high in a big gum tree with his partner, Maggie.

In Spring, Maggie lays precious white
speckled eggs in a freshly made nest.

Buckley keeps watch of passers by
and swoops anything that comes too
close to their tree home.

Maggie knows her precious eggs are
safe from harm with Buckley on guard.

Sometimes dogs wander along the
sandy path at the base of the tree.

If they dare to lift their leg to
pee on the tree...

OH DEAR!

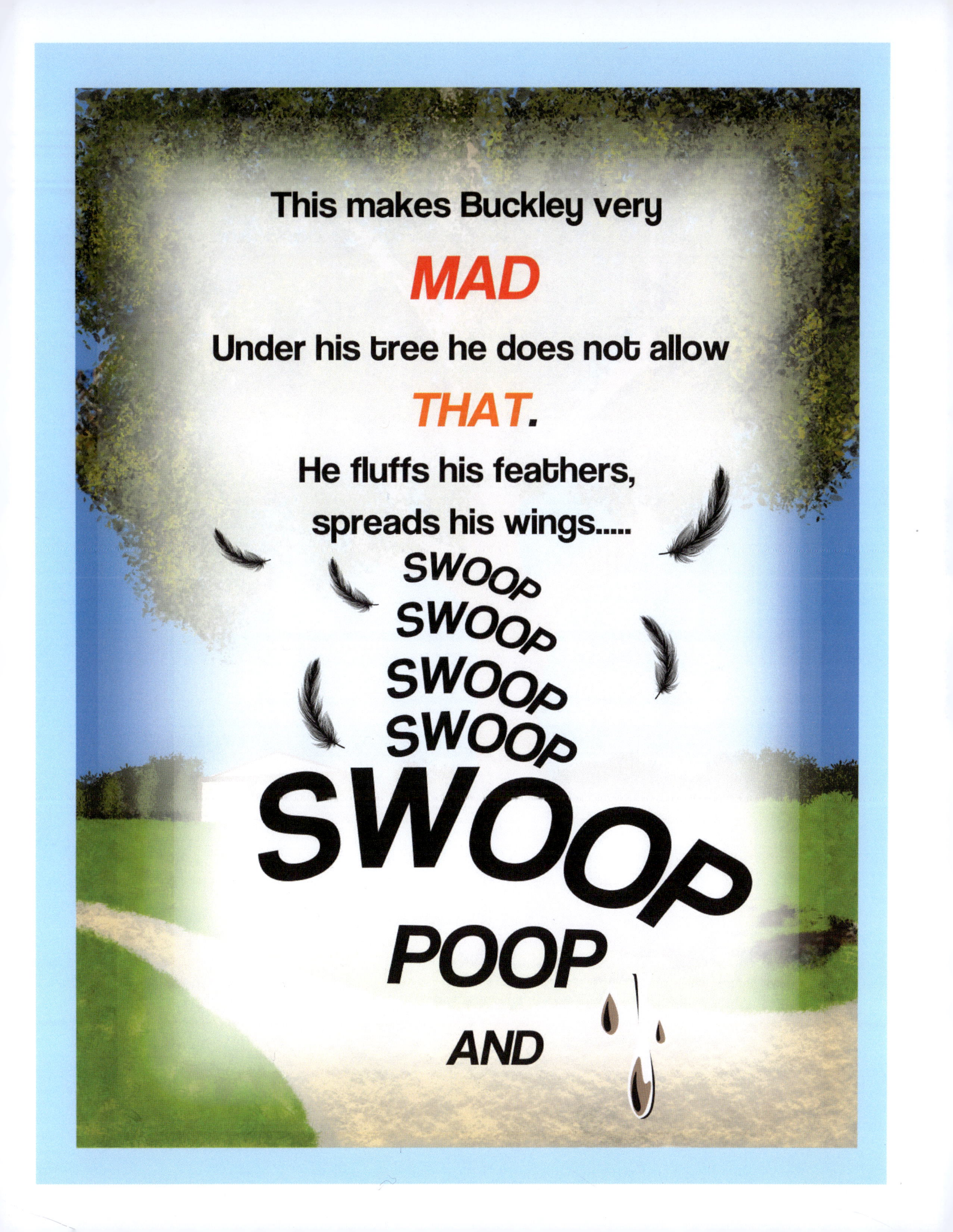

This makes Buckley very

MAD

Under his tree he does not allow

THAT.

He fluffs his feathers,

spreads his wings.....

SWOOP

SWOOP

SWOOP

SWOOP

SWOOP

POOP

AND

SPLAT!

"Run away dog and don't come back,"

Buckley squawks, as Maggie looks on proudly.

Sometimes the postie rides
by on a noisy motorcycle.

The nest shakes and the fragile eggs rattle.

This makes Buckley very

MAD

Under his tree he does not allow

THAT.

He fluffs his feathers,

spreads his wings.....

SWOOP

SWOOP

SWOOP

SWOOP

SWOOP

POOP

AND

SPLAT!

"Ride away postie and don't come back," Buckley squawks.

Feeling grateful, Maggie sings "Thank-you Buckley, you're my hero."

Sometimes drones fly above the tree,
whirring and circling.

They fly so close the air swirls.
Maggie is scared the eggs will be
blown out of the nest.

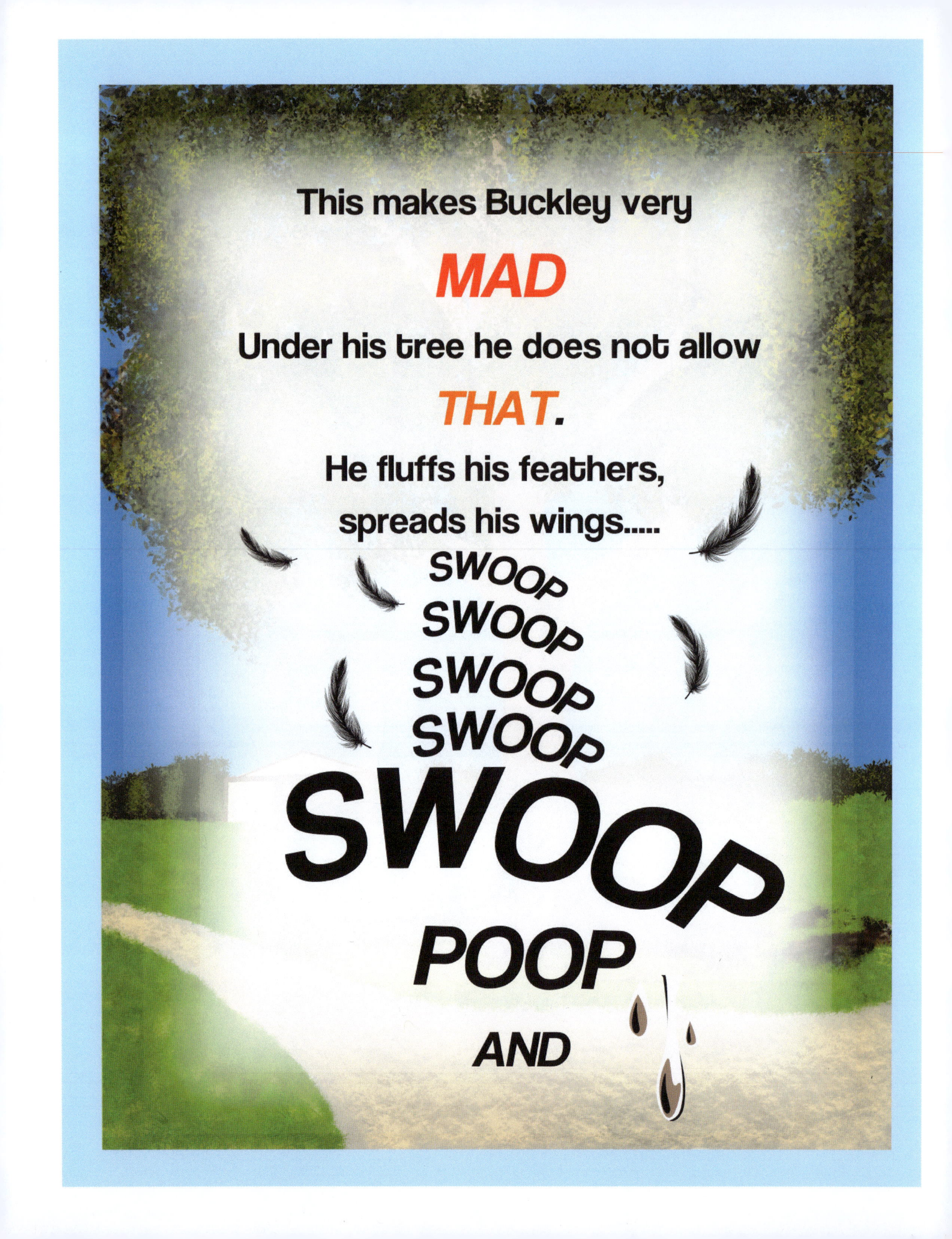

This makes Buckley very

MAD

Under his tree he does not allow

THAT.

He fluffs his feathers,

spreads his wings.....

SWOOP

SWOOP

SWOOP

SWOOP

SWOOP

POOP

AND

SPLAT!

"Fly away drone and don't come back,"
Buckley squawks.

Maggie gives him a Hi-5. "Well done Buckley, you're the best."

Some nights pesky possums crawl up the trunk of the tree toward the nest.

They are hungry and they want to eat the delicious eggs.

This makes Buckley very

MAD

Under his tree he does not allow

THAT.

He fluffs his feathers,

spreads his wings.....

SWOOP

SWOOP

SWOOP

SWOOP

SWOOP

POOP

AND

SPLAT!

"Crawl away possum and don't come back,"

Buckley squawks.

Maggie is always grateful to have Buckley looking after her and the babies.

One day a little girl named Kaley, walked slowly toward the tree, stopped, looked up at the nest and held out her hand.

Maggie could see something in Kaley's hand and wondered if she was about to throw it at the nest.

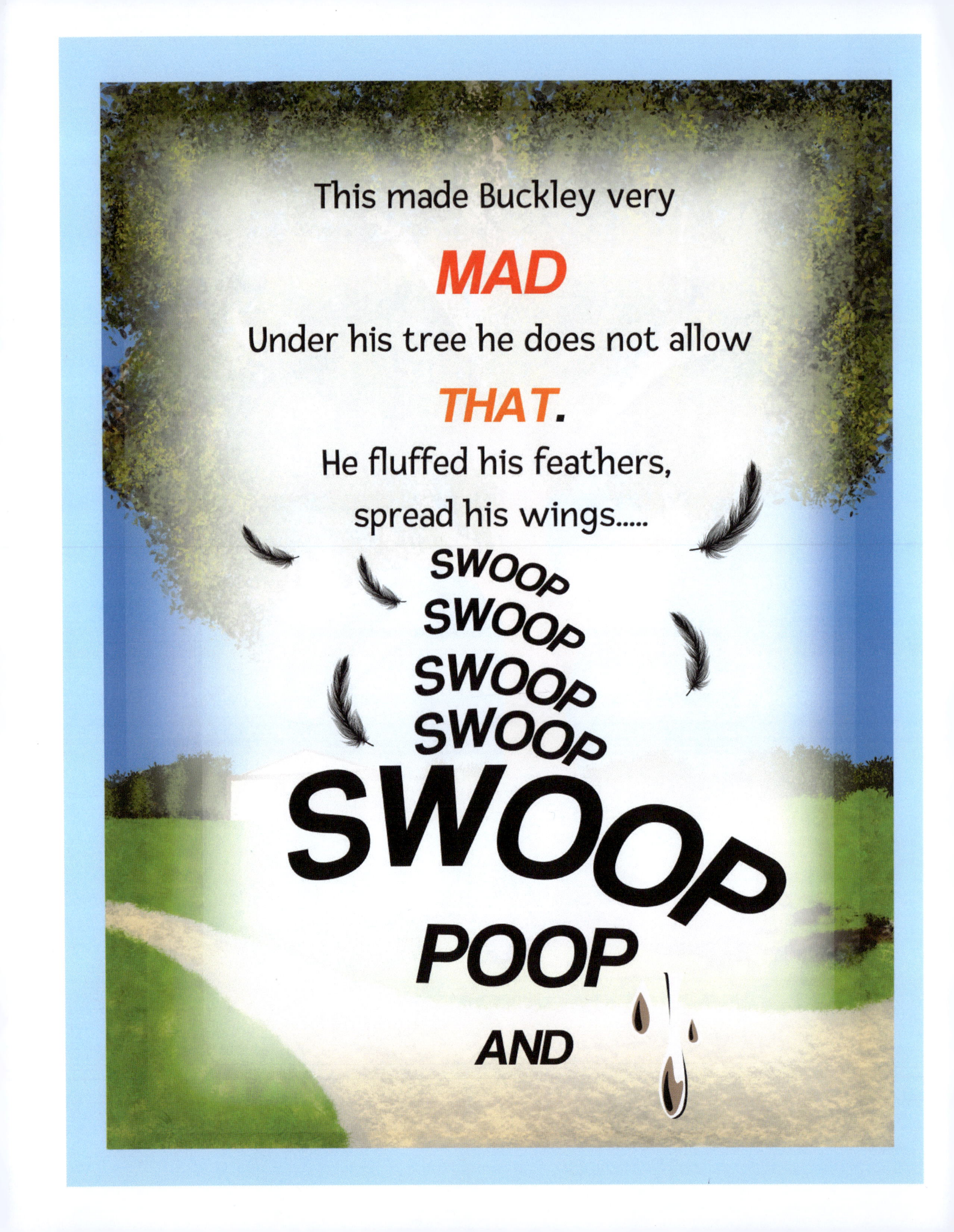

This made Buckley very

MAD

Under his tree he does not allow

THAT.

He fluffed his feathers,

spread his wings.....

SWOOP

SWOOP

SWOOP

SWOOP

SWOOP

POOP

AND

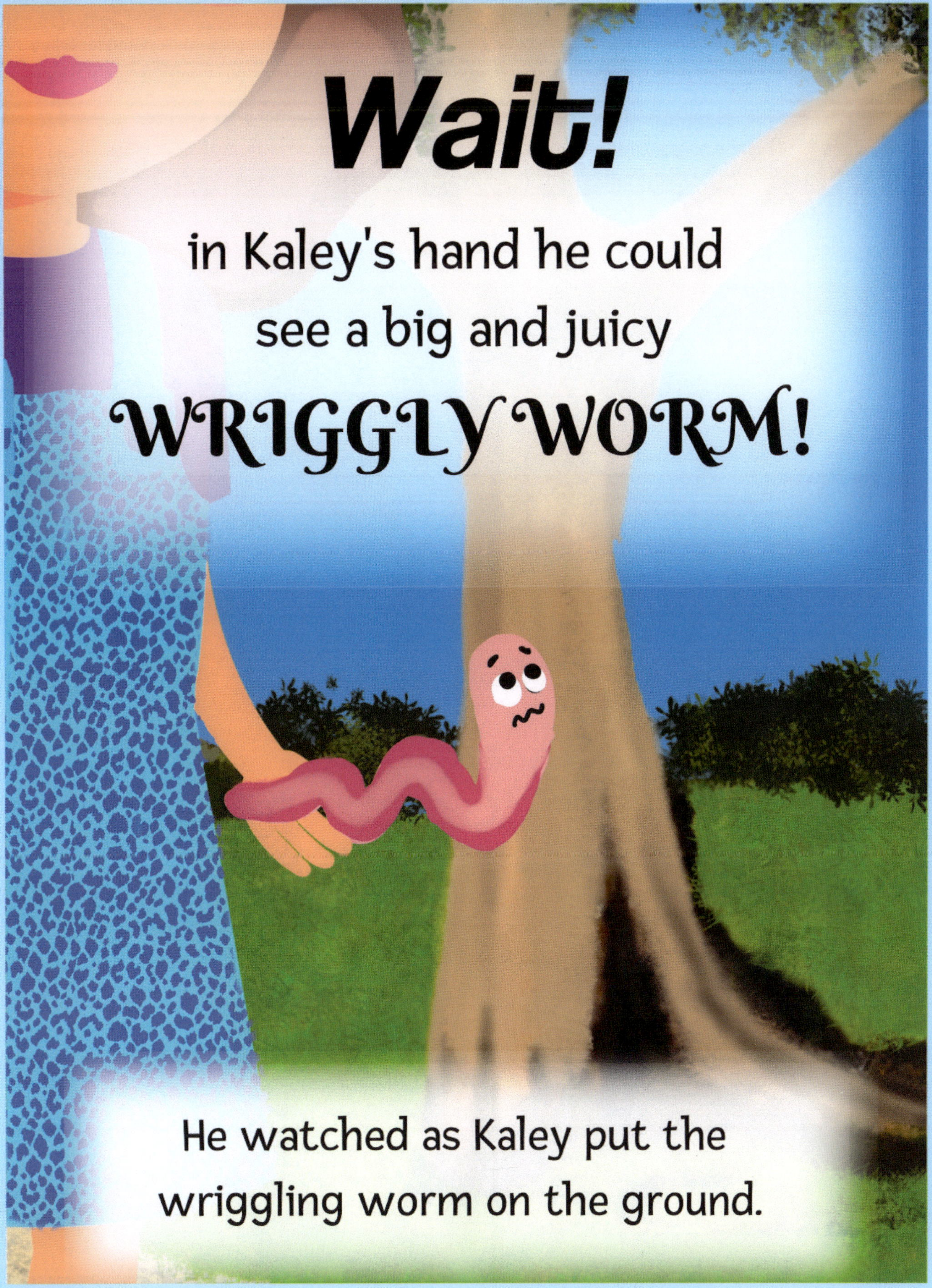

Wait!

in Kaley's hand he could
see a big and juicy
WRIGGLY WORM!

He watched as Kaley put the
wriggling worm on the ground.

He called to Maggie, then cautiously they swooped down and ate the worm.

It was

JUICY

and

DELICIOUS

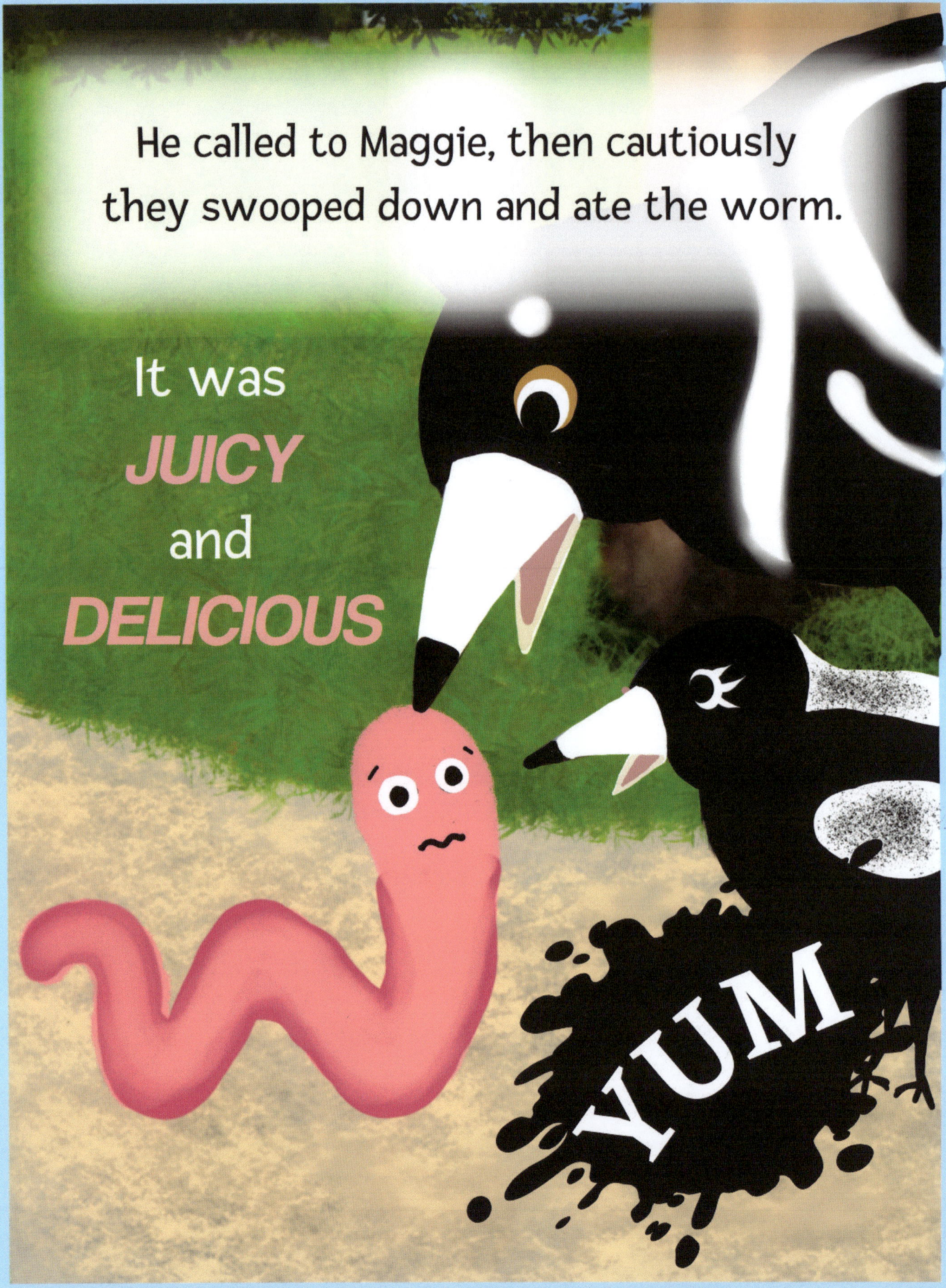

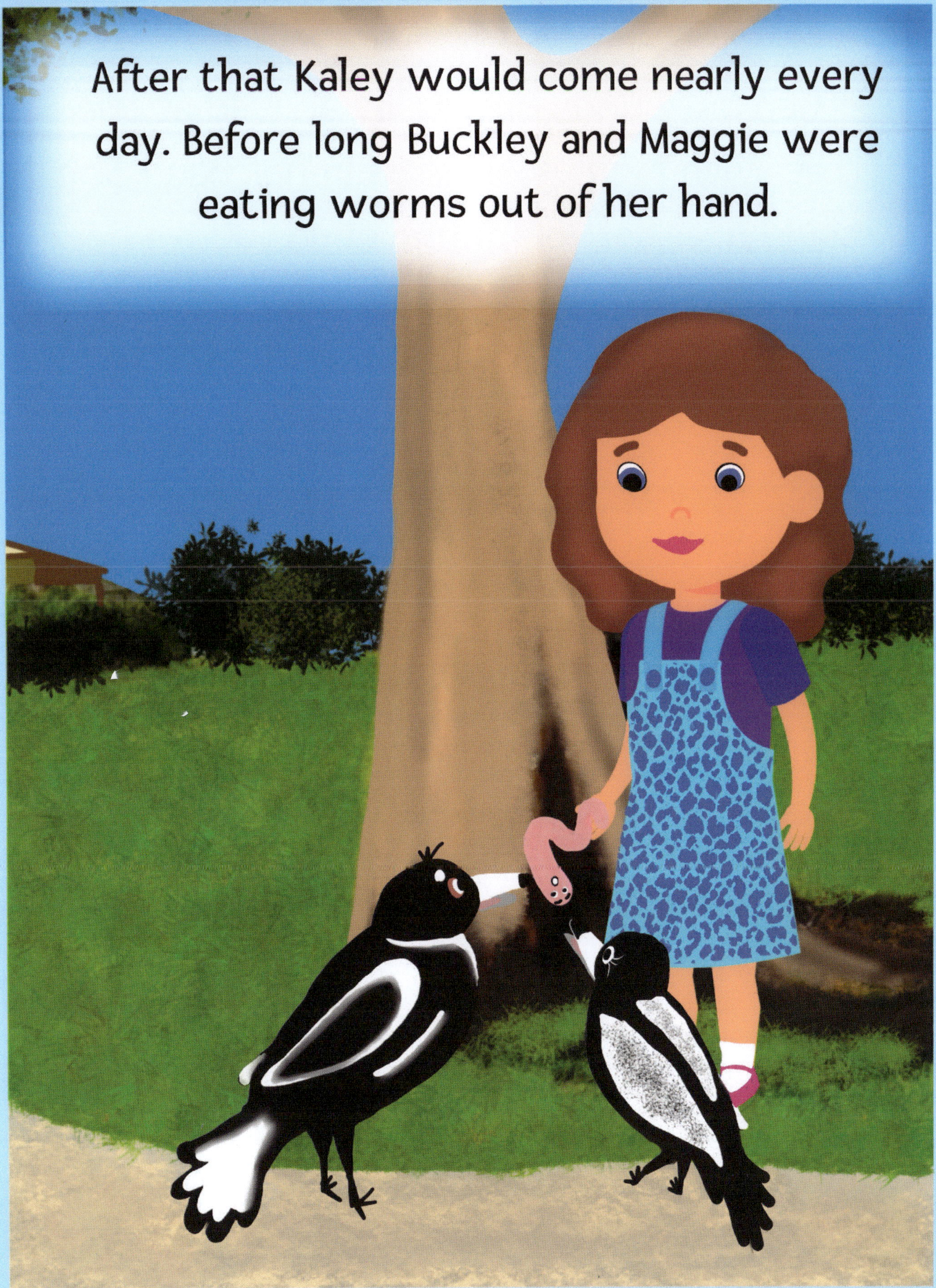
After that Kaley would come nearly every day. Before long Buckley and Maggie were eating worms out of her hand.

Then one sunny day, Kaley arrived at the tree with two big worms in her hand. She could hear soft chirping sounds above her.

Kaley looked up to see three tiny baby Magpies in the nest, their sparkling eyes curiously peeking at her.

Kaley gasped. turned, and ran away. Buckley and Maggie were confused. They were looking forward to sharing the big worms with their baby chicks.

Would their friend come back?

A short time later they saw Kaley skipping back toward their tree, with a yellow bucket in her hand.

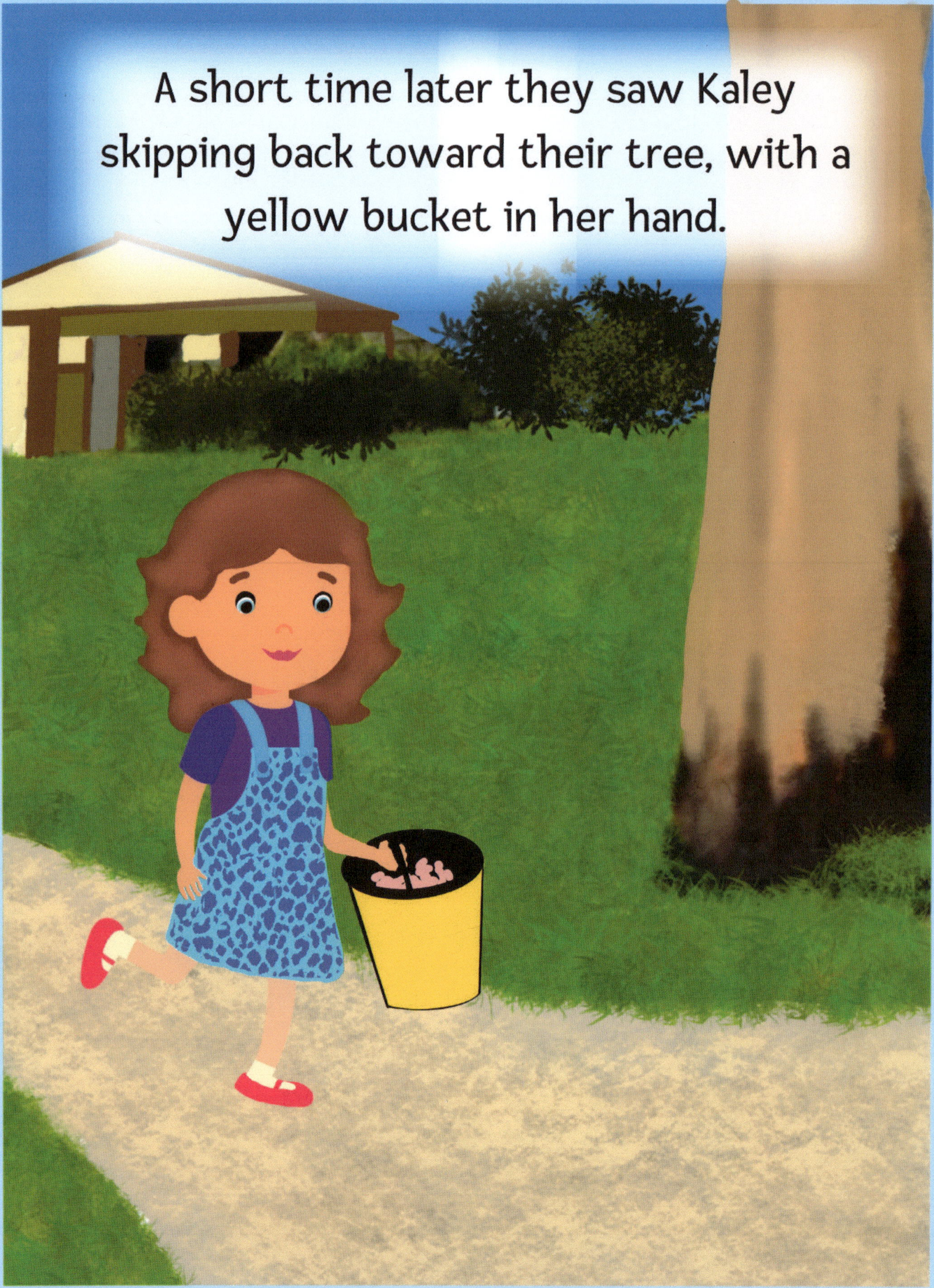

She stopped at the base of the tree and turned the bucket upside down.

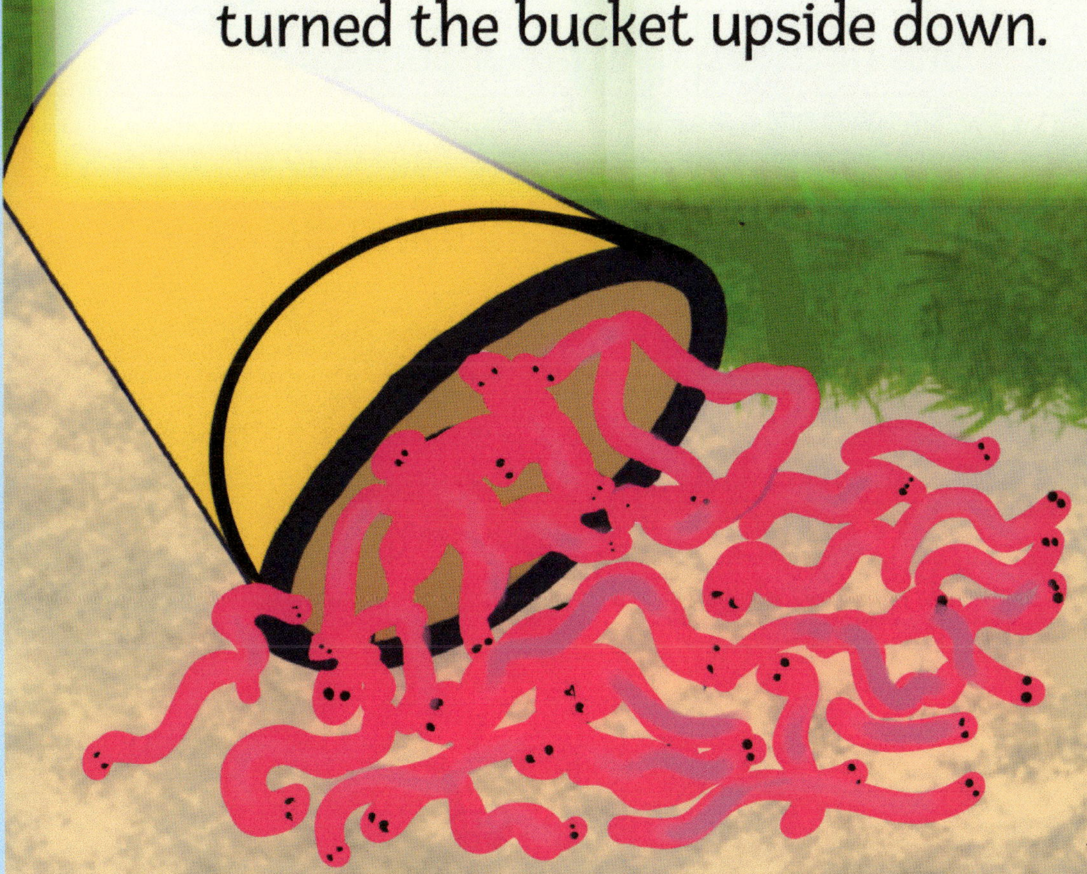

PLOP

A BIG pile of squirmy wriggling juicy worms landed on the ground.

Buckley and Maggie could not believe their eyes. What a feast!

They were about to fly down when two children. walking along the path, stopped at the tree. They looked at Kaley and the pile of worms and laughed.

One of them ran up and pushed Kaley so that she landed face first in the squirmy wormy squishy wriggly mound.

Kaley sat up, and began wiping the worms off her sad face.

This made Buckley

very

very

very

very

MAD

Madder than he had ever been before!

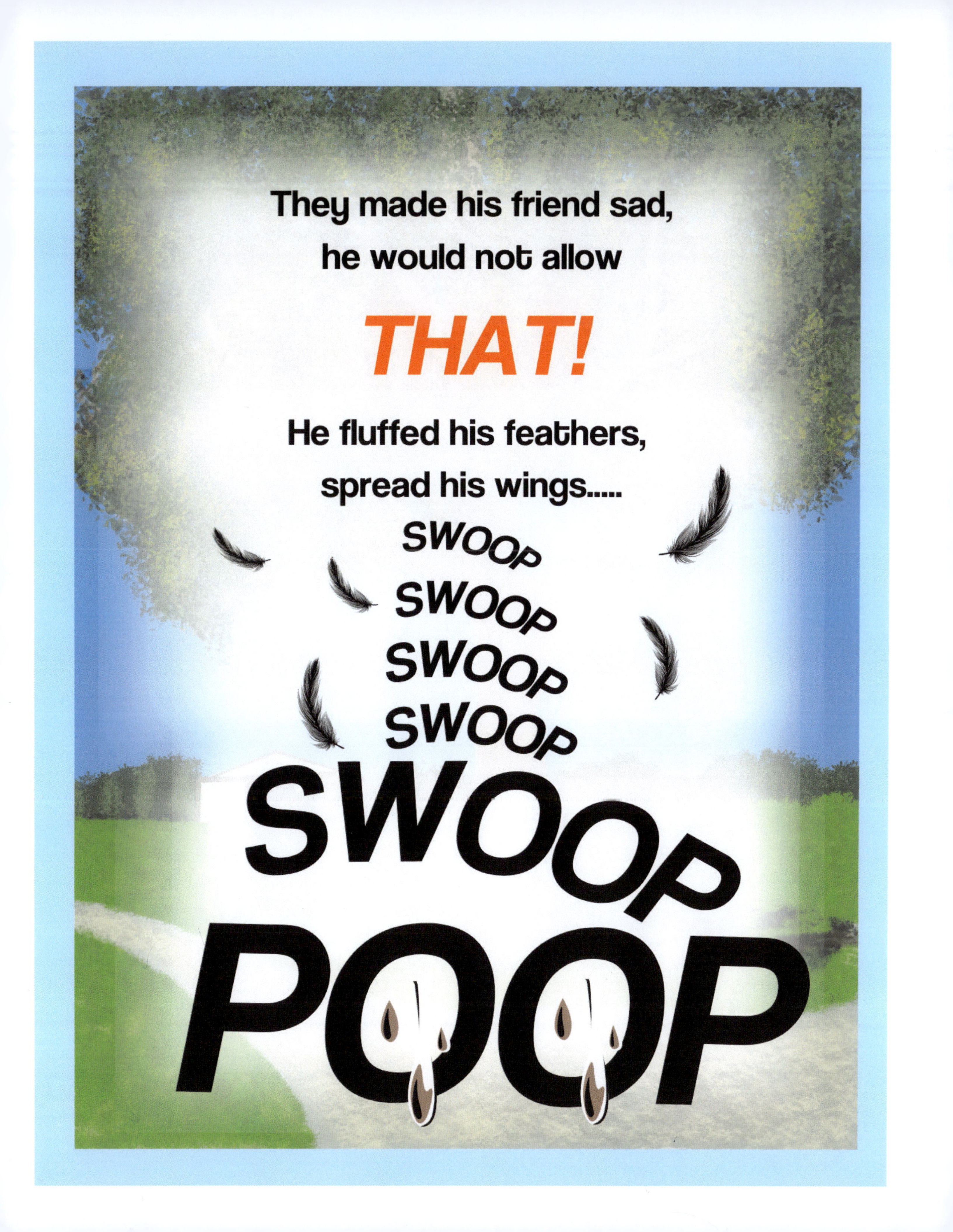

They made his friend sad,
he would not allow

THAT!

He fluffed his feathers,
spread his wings.....

SWOOP
SWOOP
SWOOP
SWOOP

SWOOP

POOP

The poop bomb EXPLODED out of Buckley's bottom.

SPLAT!

It was the

BIGGEST
poo Buckley had
EVER done.

You couldn't see the children under
the gooey slimy white slop.

Buckley landed on Maggie's shoulders and stared angrily at the two poop mounds with legs.

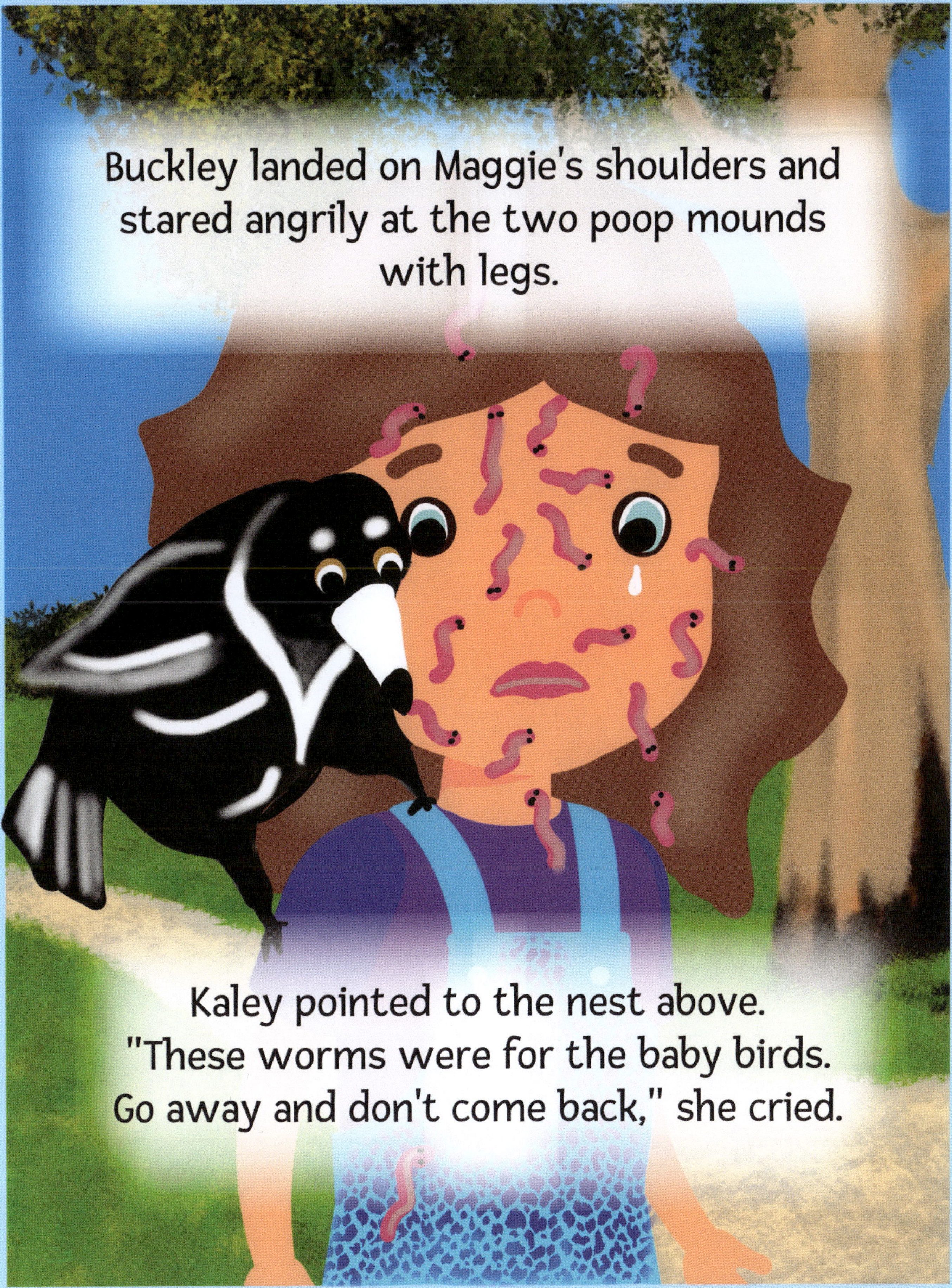

Kaley pointed to the nest above. "These worms were for the baby birds. Go away and don't come back," she cried.

The children ran away as fast as they could ."They look like snowmen" Kaley said and giggled as she wiped the tears and worms from her face.

The next day Kaley, Buckley and Maggie saw the same two children approaching the tree again. They were carrying a bucket.

Buckley spread his wings getting ready to swoop. "Don't come any closer" Kaley warned them.

They stopped and called out nervously "We're sorry about yesterday and we'd like to help"

Then they tipped the bucket they were carrying upside down. Out spilled a pile of juicy wriggly worms.

"We can bring some every day if we can just use this path to get to school" they pleaded.

"Magpies remember faces forever." Kaley informed them."So if you're kind to them and their family, they'll be kind to you."

We'll be kind, we promise." they said and with relief continued walking along the path past the tree.

Kaley climbed the tree and sat next to the chicks. She felt happy and grateful to have special Magpie friends.

Then along came a CAT!
“Hey Buckley we have a visitor,” Kaley said with a big smile and Buckley took flight.
“Here we go again” Kaley giggled.

I think you know what happened next!

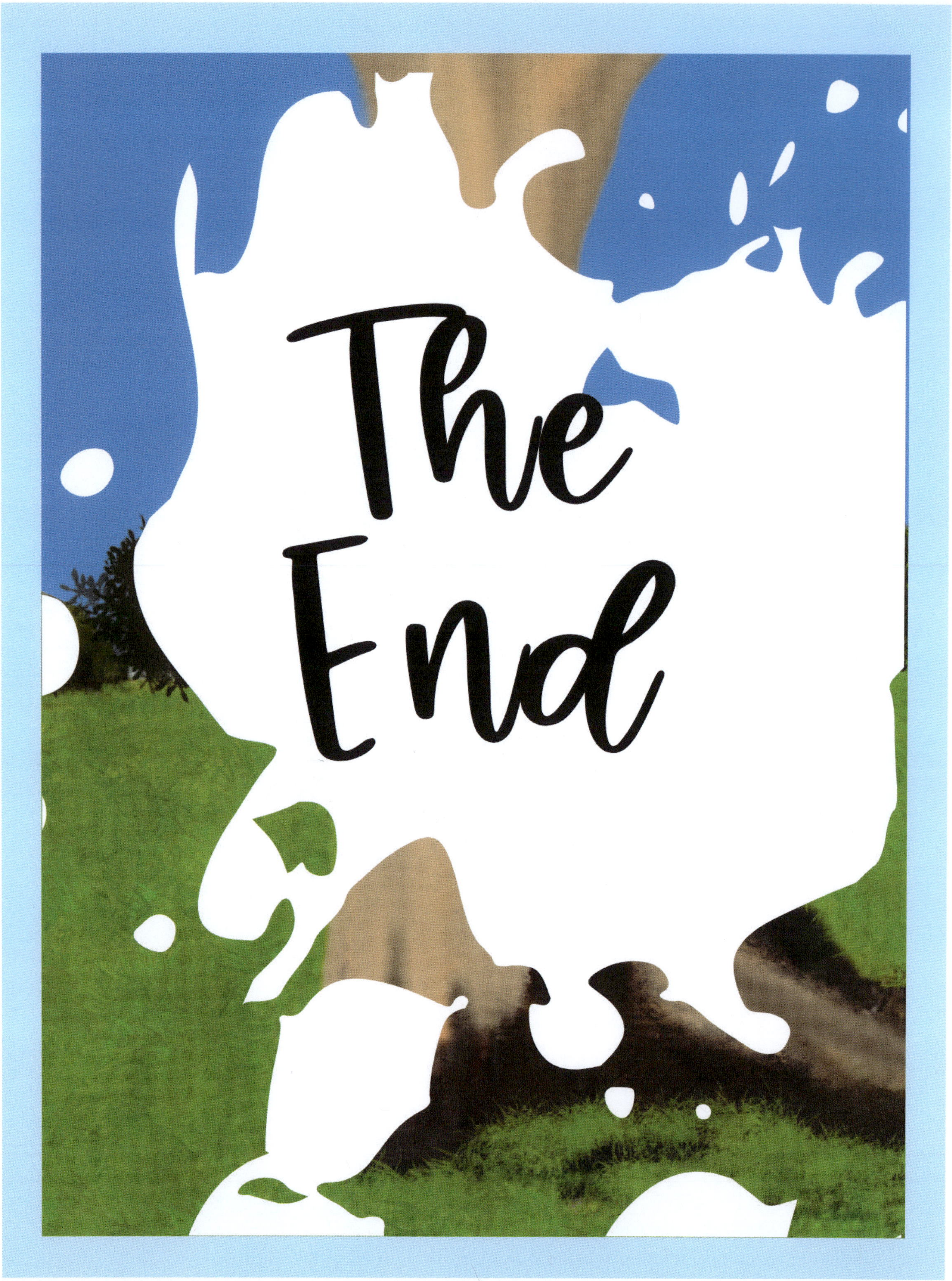
The End

Printed in Great Britain
by Amazon

48465858R00030